VICTORIAN STAINED GLASS

Trevor Yorke

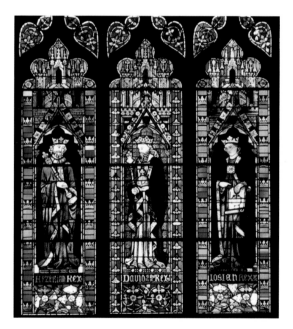

SHIRE PUBLICATIONS

Bloomsbury Publishing Plc

Kemp House, Chawley Park, Cumnor Hill, Oxford
OX2 9PH, UK

29 Earlsfort Terrace, Dublin 2, Ireland

1385 Broadway, 5th Floor, New York, NY 10018, USA

E-mail: shire@bloomsbury.com

www.shirebooks.co.uk

SHIRE is a trademark of Osprey Publishing Ltd

First published in Great Britain in 2022

A catalogue record for this book is available from the
British Library.

ISBN: PB 978 1 78442 483 1
          eBook 978 1 78442 486 2
          ePDF 978 1 78442 485 5
          XML 978 1 78442 484 8

22 23 24 25 26   10 9 8 7 6 5 4 3 2 1

Typeset by PDQ Digital Media Solutions, Bungay, UK.

Printed and bound in India by Replika Press Private Ltd.

Shire Publications supports the Woodland Trust, the
UK's leading woodland conservation charity.

COVER IMAGE

Front cover: A detail of a stained glass window
by Edward Burne-Jones in St Martin's Church,
Brampton, Cumbria, depicting St Dorothy (Alamy).
Back cover: Many early Victorian stained glass
windows illustrated biblical stories, as in this dramatic
example at Lincoln Cathedral dating from 1855,
which shows the moment when God sent an angel to
stop Abraham sacrificing his son (© Trevor Yorke).

TITLE PAGE IMAGE

The west window of Lincoln Cathedral was created
by the Sutton brothers, clerics and part-time glass
designers. When installed in 1860, stylised figures set
beneath architectural canopies was a popular design.

CONTENTS PAGE IMAGE

A detail from one of a series of four dramatic stained
glass windows in Birmingham Anglican Cathedral
by Edward Burne-Jones, a close friend of William
Morris, who is widely regarded as one of the finest ever
exponents of the art.

ACKNOWLEDGEMENTS

All illustrations other than the front cover
(and page 20, © Joanna Yorke), © Trevor Yorke.

CONTENTS

STAINED GLASS LOST AND REDISCOVERED: 1530s–1815

S TAINED GLASS WINDOWS are an inspiring, beautiful and rewarding form of art. Their kaleidoscopic colours form vibrant designs which sparkle in the sun and embellish the interior with a bewitching light, displaying the skills of leading artists and craftsmen from across the centuries. These designers had to make them both a functional part of the building that would complement the architecture, while at the same time creating images that would inspire an illiterate congregation to follow a righteous path. Stained glass windows therefore display not only the changing styles of art over the past millennium, but also unlock a treasure trove of history by revealing much about the men and women who designed and commissioned them.

Despite their aesthetic beauty, stained glass windows have a history scaling from periods of high creativity to those of reckless destruction. The message so artistically presented to one generation was viewed as blasphemous by another, while changes in architectural style and technological developments made once-fashionable colourful mosaics seem suddenly out of place. As a result, stained glass windows from the medieval period are rare and often fragmented, but are treasured for their artistic and historic value. The majority found today in cathedrals, churches or private houses date from the nineteenth and twentieth centuries, when the art form was revived. Victorian artists and designers not only created myriad colourful designs, but also had to rediscover the ways in which

OPPOSITE
This dramatic, enamel-painted apocalypse window at St Andrew's Church, Redbourne, Lincolnshire dates from the 1830s and seems to be intended to frighten the congregation into avoiding sin by displaying the horrors they would face if they did not.

The Victorians meticulously studied medieval stained glass in order to accurately recreate them and then later inspire new forms and styles, as in this beautifully detailed example from Holy Trinity Church, Blatherwycke, Northamptonshire.

the windows were originally constructed. In order to appreciate the task that faced them, it is first useful to understand how stained glass was made, why it fell from favour and what the changes were that inspired its revival.

Traditional hand-blown or antique glass has been produced in Britain since the Roman period. It was made from silicon dioxide, usually in the form of sand. As this melts at around 1500 degrees Celsius, a flux was required, for instance soda ash, so this would happen at a much lower temperature, which was achievable in ancient kilns. The molten glass produced is soluble in water, rendering it useless as a window material so a stabiliser, for instance limestone, was added to counter this. In order to form sheets of glass suitable for glazing, a number of methods were developed. Muff or cylinder glass was made by fixing a lump of molten glass to the end of a pipe, which was then blown and swung until it formed an elongated balloon shape. It was then removed from the pipe, had the ends cut off, and the remaining cylinder was sliced along its length and flattened out to make a single sheet. Crown glass was formed by blowing and rolling the tube with the molten glass at one end to form a bubble. An iron rod was then inserted at the other side and the blow pipe detached, with the glass then spun to form a flat disc which was cut up to form the small panes known as quarries. As the molten glass cooled, the outer surface solidified before the core, which could cause it to crack, so the temperature was lowered gently over a number of days in a process called annealing.

Coloured glass was created by adding metallic oxides before the initial firing in the kiln. Iron oxide could be used for yellow, cobalt for blue, copper for green and gold for reds. These were added to the silica, soda and lime mix and fired in a clay pot within the kiln; hence, this is known as pot metal glass. A problem with some colours, especially ruby red, was that the glass was too opaque. A method called flashing was therefore devised, in which a molten bubble of clear glass was dipped in red glass to leave a thin coating that was more translucent. Glaziers soon realised that by using acid to etch away the flashed coat they could create a new effect called abrading. The vast majority of the windows we see today comprise coloured rather than stained glass, the latter being a term that only became popular in the Victorian period. Stained glass actually refers to a method introduced in the early fourteenth century, when it was discovered that by applying silver nitrate to clear glass and then firing it again in a kiln it created a yellow stain. This was useful for British glaziers, as only clear glass was produced in Britain; coloured glass had to be imported from France or the Rhineland.

The final stage was to add the lines and shading to the pieces of glass with a dark brown or black paint made from iron or copper oxide and ground glass, before the finished image was fired again in the kiln. Many later medieval windows used clear glass with just dark painted outlines and shading, known as grisaille glass, from the French for grey, often with yellow stain for highlights. The strips of lead known as cames that held the glazing in place had a H-shaped profile, into which the pieces of glass were slotted and then cemented. Larger openings had additional support from iron

An example from the rare fifteenth-century medieval windows at Holy Trinity Church, Long Melford, Suffolk. Many medieval windows were later damaged and have since been reset with many fragments in random patterns.

saddle bars and stanchions – metal rods embedded in the surrounding masonry – which were usually connected to the lead cames by soldered wire.

The earliest pieces of stained glass discovered in Britain can be found at The Bede Museum, Jarrow Hall, South Tyneside, which were uncovered at the nearby monastery and probably date from the late seventh century, when it was recorded that the abbot ordered glass and glaziers from France. The oldest complete windows date from the late twelfth century, with the finest examples at York Minster and Canterbury Cathedral; ones that would later inspire Victorian designers. Over the following centuries, styles changed and techniques evolved, but stained glass windows remained a key element in the design of most churches until Henry VIII's founding of the Protestant Church of England and the Dissolution of the Monasteries in the 1530s heralded a period of neglect and destruction. The images of Christ, the Virgin Mary, apostles and saints were revered Catholic idols that Protestants rejected, on the basis that in the Second Commandment God instructs that idols or any representation of him should not be made. Henry's son, Edward VI, passed legislation ordering that 'monuments of feigned miracles, pilgrimages, idolatry and superstition', including windows, should be removed. In strongly Protestant areas some windows were lost; in others, a compromise of whitewashing the offending image might have sufficed. However, the high cost of

Maurice Johnson of Ayscoughfee Hall, Spalding, Lincolnshire, was a lawyer and founder of one of the first gentlemen's clubs in 1710. He was fascinated by old stained glass and had some of his collection set in this window, which can still be seen at his home today.

re-glazing the damaged windows was soon appreciated, so under Elizabeth I stained glass gained a degree of protection. During the English Civil War in the 1640s, puritanical Parliamentarians, who viewed idolatry as a sin and the work of the Devil, set about destroying the surviving images in windows. Some were removed or received protection; others escaped because they were high up in the church or in remote parts of the country and out of reach of the iconoclasts. However, in Scotland and Ireland the destruction was more thorough, and virtually no medieval glass has survived here.

The sudden loss of these colourful mosaic glass designs was not simply due to religious changes. The Renaissance began to influence design in Britain from the early sixteenth century, so that themes in art became more secular, with accurate representations of people, buildings in true perspective and more naturalistic landscapes. These pictures could now be created on plain windows using enamel paints made from finely crushed coloured glass mixed with borax or a similar flux, which was applied to the clear glass and then fired in a kiln to make the image permanent. This shift in technique was made more universal in 1636, when King Louis XIII's troops destroyed the glass furnaces of Lorraine – one of the main sources of coloured glass in Europe. Soon it became fashionable for churches to have large, clear glass windows designed to maximise light on plain interiors so the congregation would focus upon the spoken word from

Occasionally, enamel-painted glass was commissioned for churches during the eighteenth century and usually based on popular paintings from the period. This example is from the glorious Baroque Great Witley Parish Church, Witley Court, Worcestershire.

William Price was the youngest of three generations of glass painters working with enamels during the eighteenth century. This geometric design, believed to be by him, features in the wonderful Rococo interior of St John's Church, Shobdon, Hereford.

the pulpit. Hence, by the turn of the eighteenth century, medieval stained glass windows were viewed as old fashioned, and the skills to make pot metal glass and form the mosaic designs were now lost.

The revival in the use of stained glass began in the homes of the wealthy. Gentlemen of the Tudor and Stuart periods installed colourful coats of arms or decorative glass roundels within the windows of their properties. By the turn of the eighteenth century, there was no place for stained glass in the public parts of the new Classical-style country houses, yet there were some who found this old stained glass interesting and acquired random pieces as part of their collection of curiosities. The antiquarian William Stukeley noted that medieval windows were still being destroyed in his time and recorded on one occasion in 1736, 'I saw a cart load of painted glass, just taken from St George's church windows to put clear glass in the room. I used my influence with Mr Exton, and got the glass.'

Around this time romantic paintings featuring a ruined abbey or castle became fashionable, and gentlemen began erecting Gothic-style follies in their country parks. Horace Walpole, the son of Britain's first Prime Minister, took this a stage further and converted Strawberry Hill, a small villa high above the Thames at Twickenham, into a Gothic mansion. His vision was inspired by surviving buildings such as Westminster Abbey and was recreated by his close circle of advisors, whom he called his 'Committee for Taste', resulting in a whimsical arrangement of Gothic elements. To create the ambience he sought for his interiors, Walpole bought hundreds of decorative roundels and old pieces of coloured medieval glass to be fitted in the windows. He also commissioned two of the leading glass painters of the period – William Price the Younger and William Peckitt of York – to repaint worn pieces and create new ones to enhance his collection. Walpole also commissioned glass from James Pearson, who had worked under Price and painted the spectacular Brazen Serpent in the Wilderness window that can still be seen in Salisbury Cathedral.

Despite this dawning of interest in stained glass, many medieval windows were still being replaced by clear glass or enamel-painted replicas. Even a leading architect like James Wyatt was guilty of such a crime when he was called in to remodel Salisbury Cathedral in 1789. He proceeded to have the remaining medieval windows smashed up in order to remove the valuable lead, with the centuries-old stained glass simply dumped in a ditch. Yet, only seventy years later, much of his work was being removed and old mosaic-style windows made from pot metal glass were being commissioned in their place. This sudden shift in the design of stained glass from painted enamels to a revival of true medieval styles was inspired by a religious and architectural revolution at the dawn of the Victorian period.

BELOW LEFT
An example of one of the roundels at Strawberry Hill. Sixteenth- and seventeenth-century glass like this became fashionable in the early nineteenth century.

BELOW RIGHT
Repairing windows in cathedrals helped to keep a few glass painters in business, including William Peckitt. He created this armorial glass at Lincoln Cathedral.

INGRESSA SVNT AD NOE IN ARCA OANIO

THE GOTHIC REVIVAL: 1815–1860

IN THE ECONOMIC gloom that followed the conclusion of the Napoleonic Wars in 1815, the ruling classes had genuine fears of revolution. One solution to quell this threat was to address the waning influence of the Church of England, principally the issue that it had failed to adapt to the shift of population towards urban and industrial areas. Old parishes began to be reorganised and a new generation of government-funded edifices was erected under the watchful eye of commissioners. Many of these new commissioner churches embraced the rising interest in the Gothic, with tall pointed windows sometimes filled with stained glass. In addition to this boom in Anglican church building, legislative changes ended centuries of persecution and denial of positions of power for Roman Catholics and they too began erecting their own places of worship.

By the 1830s many in the Church of England were advocating the adoption of aspects of medieval traditions into the Anglican Liturgy. The Oxford Movement founded by John Keble in 1833 and the Cambridge Camden Society formed in 1839 were influential in changing the design and style of the new churches being built. Gone were the plain whitewashed walls and clear windows; back came colour and mystery enhanced by the reintroduction of stained glass.

The Gothic Revival that these changes ignited was fine-tuned by the architect and designer Augustus Welby Northmore Pugin. This passionate medievalist was invigorated

OPPOSITE
This window in Ely Cathedral by Alfred Gérente comprises a column of roundels depicting the story of Noah. The bright primary colours and stylised figures are distinctive of windows of the 1850s.

by the colour and ceremonial drama of the Catholic church to which he converted; a contemporary biographer, Benjamin Ferrey, recorded, 'it was attractive to his imaginative mind.' He promoted Gothic as the correct form of Christian architecture and that those seeking to work in the style should not just copy the forms but understand the methods originally used to create it. In his own works, which included commissions for numerous Catholic clients and the interiors of the new Houses of Parliament, he encouraged leading glaziers of the day to produce authentic medieval stained glass. The exacting standards that he demanded resulted in a turbulent relationship with some, but helped drive the rediscovery of the lost skills required to create them.

While Pugin and the Cambridge Camden Society were beginning their campaign to revive authentic medieval stained

A window
in Chester
Cathedral
attributed to
John Hardman
and Augustus
Pugin and dating
from around
1850. Figures
set beneath
architectural
canopies with
a broad range
of colours
as seen here
would become
fashionable by
the end of the
decade.

glass, the majority of new windows were still enamel paintings on thin, smooth sheets of clear or pale-coloured glass. The figures were usually dressed in a toga with deep folded fabric and had faces that were round with petite mouths, pronounced chins and wide oval eyes. The background usually featured either a simple pattern or a picture of a Classical-style landscape or building. As the shading was built up by applying more layers of paint, parts of the picture could appear almost black as they blocked light passing through. Enamel paint was fired onto the glass at lower temperatures than pot metal glass and was hence more prone to deterioration.

These early Victorian enamel painters were usually not trained artists but had developed their skills from work as a plumber or glazier, as both involved working with lead. As a result many of the figures in surviving painted glass windows from the 1830s are rather amateur and lack the finesse of contemporary fine art. A notable exception was Thomas Willement, who was one of the first to view the medium as a mosaic of coloured glass rather than a painting. He produced windows for Pugin, but the great designer was not satisfied and looked elsewhere; however, with the increasing demand for

ABOVE RIGHT This window by David Evans at St Chad's Church, Shrewsbury, has the glass cut into shapes to complement the design rather than just painted on a sheet. His work marks a transition from the enamel glass painters to the revival of medieval stained glass.

An example of an 1857 window comprising columns of medallions or roundels at Holy Trinity Church, Blatherwycke, Northamptonshire. Some windows of this type used just geometric designs in the roundels.

windows for new churches Willement's order book remained full and he became a wealthy man.

The next step in the recreation of medieval windows came from a lawyer, Charles Winston, who had a passion for stained glass. He worked with scientists to study the chemical composition of old pieces of glass and convinced a leading glass manufacturer, James Powell and Sons, to reproduce it using the correct metal oxides. Winston also realised that the richness of medieval glazing was due to its irregularities and hence he recommended the use of hand-blown crown and cylinder glass, which refracted the light, rather than the flat and lacklustre contemporary glass.

By the 1850s these discoveries enabled glaziers to recreate medieval windows with individual pieces of authentic pot metal glass arranged in mosaic leaded designs. A popular form in this period featured a column of roundels or medallions set on a mosaic background of vivid blues, reds and bright greens. The window would depict a biblical story read from the bottom up, with these narrative windows often referred to today as a 'Poor Man's Bible'. Other windows had a scene from an Old or a New Testament story filling up each light. The figures were based upon the stylised artwork from medieval windows, manuscripts or carvings, with simple outlines and little shading. They are often curvilinear in stance with exaggerated poses and elongated limbs. Ripples in their clothes are in bold black so they appear almost two dimensional.

Many of the designers and glass painters who emerged in the 1850s had a more artistic background than their predecessors. The son of an architect, George Hedgeland was a talented draughtsman in his own right, with Charles Winston stating that his designs demonstrated 'the enormous superiority of an artist over the herd of glass-Wrights'. His finest pieces, which can still be seen today, are the east windows at Norwich Cathedral and Halifax Minster. Unfortunately, Hedgeland's career was cut short by bad health and he sold up and emigrated to Australia in 1860. Michael O'Connor began his career as a painter of heraldic glass in the studio of Thomas Willement. After a spell back in Ireland, he returned to England and worked alongside his son Arthur, producing work for Pugin at St Saviour's Church, Leeds, and for

By the late 1850s some windows had a single design spread across a row of lights, as in this example by Thomas Baillie at St Nicholas Church, Montgomery, Powys, Wales. The fragmented deep blue sky with gold stars was also fashionable.

All Saints, Margaret Street, a Gothic masterpiece by William Butterfield, hidden away behind Oxford Street, London. He had to give up his work due to failing eyesight in the late 1850s. One of the finest designers of the period was Francis Wilson Oliphant, who trained at the Edinburgh Academy of Art and studied ecclesiastical artwork before setting up his own studio in 1855. He sought to improve his glass through involvement in production as well as the design, but died prematurely only four years later.

In this window at Chester Cathedral, c.1859, the designer, believed to be Michael O'Connor, has treated the window as one large canvas, an approach that would become common in the following decades.

The Great Exhibition in 1851 gave many of this first generation of stained glass designers an opportunity to display their work for a global audience. Yet, despite their improvements, there were still enamel-painted pieces and glass of poor quality on display, and much of it was inferior to revival work from the continent. Just over ten years later, however, at the International Exhibition of 1862 at South Kensington, London, the rapid technical and stylistic developments of the previous decade resulted in British stained glass being among the finest in the world. These improvements were in part driven by a notable increase in demand, one that encouraged existing glazing firms to expand and new studios to be established such that the 1860s would be dominated by the work of these successful companies.

ABOVE RIGHT
This window dating from the late 1850s at Peterborough Cathedral still has medieval stylised figures, but the design is full of movement and the colours are subtle – features more indicative of windows from the next decade.

VICTORIAN STAINED GLASS COMPANIES: THE 1860s

THE 1860s MARK the high point of the Gothic Revival, when the style permeated most types of new building. Anglican churches and chapels were being erected to spread the faith to the industrialised masses or remote farming communities alongside those raised for Catholic worship and the restorations being made to existing edifices. The demand for stained glass increased further, as from the late 1850s it became fashionable to commemorate the passing of a family member by commissioning a memorial window with their epitaph recorded in the text below it. This was a boom time for the craft, and many glazing companies and studios produced windows on an almost industrial scale. Some became large-scale enterprises employing hundreds of staff and supplying their wares across the country and abroad, while others remained small scale and primarily served a local area.

Some of these businesses were established around the work of an outstanding designer, while others paid a leading artist to create designs for their major commissions with an in-house team to deal with everyday orders. After the patron had approved the preliminary design for the project, detailed and accurate measurements of the window opening were made to create a template. From this a full-size master drawing on parchment or paper was made, known as the cartoon, which included the lead lines and the colours of each piece of glass. It was common for the cartoon to be retained and used on later projects with minor adjustments to suit different windows.

OPPOSITE
A section of the Great East Window at Bath Abbey, which depicts fifty-six scenes from the life of Christ. It is by Clayton and Bell, one of the most prolific Victorian stained glass window companies.

These portraits of Victoria and Albert have the rather stiff design, bright, garish colours and muddy pink skin tones with foliage on the plain pieces that was typical of much late-1850s and early-1860s work.

OPPOSITE
The lower corners of windows may reveal the mark of the company that made it. These examples highlighted by the white arrows are William Wailes (left), George Hedgeland (centre) and C.E. Kempe (right); the latter used a wheatsheaf symbol.

A cut line was a tracing of the cartoon made onto a sheet of translucent paper or linen which showed just the lead lines and was used for parts of the assembly. The individual pieces of coloured glass were then placed over the drawing and shaped using a cutter and trimmed with a tool called a grozing iron before the lines, shading and yellow stain were added. The leading up process involved fitting the window together like a jigsaw and slotting the pieces into the lead cames to complete each individual light before they were transported and installed on site.

Finding out which company or studio made a particular window can be surprisingly difficult. If you look closely in the bottom corners of windows you might find a signature, although some just used initials or a symbol. If there is a date it usually applied to the person whom the window commemorates, although the window itself would usually have been made within a couple of years of their death. Church records or the diocesan archives may record who paid for the window and from which company, while old newspapers could have these details in their

This striking window in Peterborough Cathedral dates from 1865 and was produced by the studio of Michael O'Connor. The wide range of rich colours is typical of the 1860s, but the lively composition with dynamic figures marks a clear change from the static design in the previous image.

reporting of the dedication service. It can be worth looking for similar-style windows in local buildings where the designer may be known or contacting a local stained glass expert or studio who may have worked on it. Also, follow the records of the patron of the building, as they might have financed other work and used the same designer for the windows in each project. If all else fails, a close study of the overall design,

stylistic details and the type of glass used – which can then be compared with other examples online – may narrow down a likely candidate. If the records of the company still exist then their involvement could be confirmed; unfortunately, many of these have been lost before their historic value was appreciated.

An example of a typical Gothic stained glass window of the 1860s by the Chance Brothers, with a broad range of bright colours seemingly selected without reference to the nature of the object it was depicting – for instance, the green and lilac on the halos and parts of the building.

Some of the leading Victorian stained glass companies were founded at an early date. The Chance Brothers from Smethwick, Birmingham, had supplied the 300,000 sheets of glass used in the construction of the Crystal Palace for the 1851 Great Exhibition and also had a department specialising in coloured glass that had displays at the event. William Warrington established his own firm in 1832 and produced some of the earliest authentic medieval-style windows, including work for Pugin before the pair fell out. Another company the great designer used was William Wailes of Newcastle. The young William was originally a grocer but built a kiln at the rear of his business to make little enamels before quitting and establishing his own studio in 1838. Wailes produced windows for Pugin, who liked his cheap prices, but looked elsewhere when he was not satisfied with the results. This had little effect on William's business, which was already booming, so that by the time of the Great Exhibition his was one of the leading companies, employing over seventy staff. The windows produced by William Wailes tend to use lighter tones than those of his contemporaries, often with a wide range of bright colours, including distinctive mauves and pinks.

Pugin encouraged his friend and fellow Catholic John Hardman to make stained glass for him, and his company produced most of his later work. Initially the drawings for his windows were sent by train from Pugin's home in Ramsgate to Hardman's works in Birmingham. This disconnection of the artist from his creation frustrated Pugin, who stated that 'we shall never produce anything good until the furnaces are within a few yards of the easel.' Despite this, Hardman's stained glass windows were of a high standard, and this continued after Pugin's premature death in 1852. Many of their windows were for new Catholic churches, but they also produced stained glass for the House of Commons as part of Pugin's designs and windows for both the Anglican and Catholic cathedrals in Sydney, Australia.

In Scotland the destruction of medieval stained glass had been more thorough and the fledgling companies that began to emerge in the first half of the nineteenth century had few original windows to inspire them and poor-quality glass to work with. Those who began producing work for new Scottish churches included William Cairney and Sons, who were established in 1828, David Keir and Sons in 1847 and Hugh Bogle and Co in 1850. Ballantine and Allan were founded in 1837 by James Ballantine and

A colourful window by William Wailes from around 1860. As with their designs from the previous decade, bright red, greens and blues dominate, with foliage patterns across the plain pieces, but now the figures fill most of each light and the canopies above are more prominent.

ERECTED TO THE MEMORY OF THE LATE   PRINCE CONSORT BY G W JOHNSON 1863

George Allan in Edinburgh. Despite the struggles they faced
in achieving their desired standard of stained glass, they still
managed to win the competition to supply windows for the
new Houses of Parliament, although in the end they only
made those for the House of Lords.

James Powell and Sons, who had worked with Charles
Winston, became a prominent name in stained glass from
the 1850s. They used numerous designers to create their
stained glass windows, including Edward Burne-Jones, Henry
Holiday, William De Morgan and Walter Crane, who would
all be influential in the coming decades. The company also
sold quarry glass – small clear panes with a printed pattern
highlighted by yellow stain. This mass-produced moulded
glass could be used to form a cheap decorative window and
was often fitted in newly built churches until money was
available later to replace it with stained glass.

By the 1860s a new generation of designers had risen to
prominence and established successful businesses that would

dominate Victorian stained glass production. Clement Heaton came from an ecclesiastical background and was trained to work on stained glass for William Holland of Warwick, where he may have met James Butler, a lead glazier working in the same area. The two formed a partnership in London that was later renamed Heaton, Butler and Bayne after the talented artist Robert Turnill Bayne joined their design team. Their work not only included the Brunel Memorial Window in Westminster Abbey but also the production of over one hundred different colours of glass, which were specially designed by Heaton to survive the British climate.

One of the most successful and prolific Victorian stained glass companies was Clayton and Bell. Unlike many of the early studios, John Clayton and Alfred Bell were both talented artists, the former producing drawings for the *London Illustrated News* and the latter a draughtsman for the leading church architect George Gilbert Scott. It was Scott who suggested the two should form a business partnership so they could produce stained glass windows for him, although with the pair's society contacts they found work easy to come by and employed around three hundred staff by 1870. As with many of the busy Victorian studios, the pair were heavily involved in the design of the windows in the early days, with Clayton specialising in the figure work and Bell the architectural canopies. However, as their commissions increased they often just sketched out the cartoon and left

OPPOSITE
A window of 1863 by Clayton and Bell with large, prominent figures, featuring multi-coloured robes surrounded by busy patterned backgrounds and finely detailed architectural canopies characteristic of this decade.

A beautiful design from 1864, probably by Nathaniel Westlake for Lavers and Barraud, in Worcester Cathedral. The colours are richer and the figures more graceful than was typical at this date. It was commissioned by local freemasons and incorporates their symbols in the lower panels.

Ward and Hughes glazed the huge east window at Lincoln Cathedral as well as this later example from 1869, most likely because Ward's brother was Dean of the cathedral.

The detailed foliage in this 1865 window at Blatherwycke, Northampton-shire, by Alexander Gibbs and Co, is more typical of the next decade.

the detailed work to others and sometimes reused the same design with small alterations for different commissions. Their army of artists and glaziers would have specialised in different elements of the window's production, with those who painted the figures generally the best paid. A criticism of this system of production by many hands is that the original artist's concept was watered down, a drop in quality which Pugin previously highlighted and which later Arts and Crafts designers would seek to resolve.

John Burlison and Thomas John Grylls had both trained at Clayton and Bell, and just like their masters were encouraged by architects to form their own stained glass company. Burlison and Grylls made its name with the new styles of

stained glass design that evolved from the 1860s, with perhaps their most spectacular piece the south rose window in Westminster Abbey of 1902. Nathaniel Wood Lavers and Francis Philip Barraud had both worked for James Powell and Sons before going into partnership together. Although Barraud designed some of their early work, they employed freelance designers for their larger commissions including Alfred Bell, Henry Stacy Marks, James Milner Allen and Henry Holiday. The company's busy in-house style evolved to more simplified and open designs in the hands of Nathaniel Hubert John Westlake, with the company renamed Lavers, Barraud and Westlake in 1868.

Most of these leading Victorian stained glass companies were based in London, but there were many other successful enterprises further afield, one of the most highly respected being Shrigley and Hunt of Lancaster. Arthur Hunt was an apprentice at Heaton, Butler and Bayne before he moved and took over Hudson and Shrigley,

a century-old decorating business in this northern city. Under his leadership they began producing stained glass windows that reflected the changing styles away from the multi-coloured and complex designs of the Gothic Revival to ones with a more restrained colour palette and simpler designs, set in more realistic surroundings.

A window by Alexander Gibbs and Co at All Saints Church, Margaret Street, London, which marks the change to simpler imagery and restrained colours from the late 1860s.

This new approach to decorative art which inspired Shrigley and Hunt, among others, had evolved from the work of another company formed in the 1860s by a group of leading artists, including a pair of Oxford graduates, William Morris and Edward Burne-Jones.

The former premises of Shrigley and Hunt opposite the Old Castle in Lancaster.

MORRIS AND Co, HOLIDAY AND KEMPE: 1870–1900

WILLIAM MORRIS WAS a rare genius: a poet, author, painter and designer with an exceptional eye for colour, who, unlike his contemporaries, believed it was important that the artist should be involved in every stage of the creation of his art. He looked to the medieval past with admiration but used it for inspiration on both an artistic and social level, stating, 'Let us study it wisely, be taught by it, kindled by it; all the while determining not to imitate or repeat it.' Morris had entered Oxford University in 1853 with the intention of training for the church but emerged four years later an artist. He was influenced by the art critic John Ruskin, who encouraged the detailed study of nature, and the Pre-Raphaelite Brotherhood, a group of young artists who had rejected the fashionable style of Classical painting for one that was more contemporary and romantic. One of their number, Dante Gabriel Rossetti, became involved in designing stained glass windows and influenced younger artists and designers like Morris who were establishing their own studios at the time.

After frustrated attempts to find suitable furnishings for his new home, The Red House in Bexleyheath, Morris and a group of associates including his close friend from Oxford, Edward Burne-Jones, formed a company. They set out to produce well-designed, quality goods for the home that would raise the standards of the decorative arts. Although they would become famous for furnishings and wallpaper design

OPPOSITE
The Ascension by Edward Burne-Jones at St Philip's Cathedral, Birmingham, divided horizontally into heaven above earth, with its striking reds making a dramatic impression as one enters this wonderful edifice.

An early Morris, Marshall and Faulkner window in Peterborough Cathedral. Their designs had simple linework with minimal shading but were richly detailed.

Morris often surrounded windows with clear, patterned glass to highlight the figure and let in more light, as here at St Martin's Church, Low Marple, Manchester.

when Morris, Marshall and Faulkner was established in 1861, the main source of income was from stained glass windows. Their designs were a product of many talented artistic hands, yet were unified in composition and detail to form a distinctive in-house style with a clear and concise manner, featuring restrained colour schemes, contemporary figures and accurately detailed flora and fauna. Edward Burne-Jones and Ford Madox Brown – who had both produced work for James Powell and Sons – did a lot of the figure work, Morris himself

Morris and Co figures had impassioned poses, with distinctive shallow 'm'-shaped top lips and wavy hair, as in this example at St Edward's Church, Leek, Staffordshire.

Morris carefully selected the colours, often in combinations of gold and green, yellow and blue or green and red, as in this example of 1873 at St Martin's Church, Low Marple, Manchester.

designed the foliage patterns and chose the colours of glass to be used, while Philip Webb, who had designed the Red House for Morris, was a dab hand at the animals.

After a regrettable falling out of the partners and the reformation of the company as Morris and Co in 1876, it would be Edward Burne-Jones who would become the leading designer of their glass and one of the most influential and greatest exponents of the art. He had received training from Rossetti, but most of his artistic skills were self-taught. His style evolved from the realism and detailed studies of the early Pre-Raphaelites to the focus on beautiful, dreamlike figures set in fantasy worlds embellished with foliage and fauna that

characterise the aesthetic movement of the 1870s. Like many of this new generation, Burne-Jones sought inspiration from international sources, with Classical as well as medieval themes involving romance and tragedy. His exceptional eye for design shines through in his stained glass windows with beautifully composed, two-dimensional arrangements like a frieze with dominant, expressive figures.

The stained glass windows of Morris and Co were an inspiration to other leading artists emerging at the time. Henry Holiday entered the Royal Academy Schools at the age of fifteen and came under the influence of Rossetti and Morris. After Burne-Jones left James Powell and Sons to help Morris establish their company in 1861, Holiday took over as chief designer and remained with them for nearly thirty years. His sources of inspiration broadened after a visit to Italy in 1867, and his windows evolved from the colourful, busy Gothic to more of a Renaissance flavour, with lively compositions of naturalistic figures and detailed foliage sometimes with Classical-style elements in the background.

Holiday produced over three hundred designs for Powell and Sons, with many used around the British Empire and the United States, reflecting how foreign demand was now an important part of a stained glass company's business. However, he regretted not escaping the restricted practice of mass production sooner and relished the freedom he found after leaving Powell and Sons in 1890 to establish his own studio. Here he could be involved in all stages of the production so as to retain the original artistic concept, a practice of craftsmanship which Pugin had so desired. In addition to his cartoons, Holiday also exhibited

A Henry Holiday window at Ely Cathedral. His beautifully drawn figures are complemented by detailed foliage in tones of green and architectural details from varied sources.

A distinctive C.E. Kempe window from All Saints Church, Bakewell, with richly dressed figures, dark coloured fabrics and a finely drawn background filled with clear and yellow glass.

his paintings, produced drawings for books written by his friend Lewis Carroll and, like Morris, was a keen socialist and later supporter of the suffragette movement.

While Holiday and Burne-Jones filled their windows with aesthetically beautiful figures, Charles Eamer Kempe created a distinctive style that was luxuriously detailed with a draughtsman-like quality. Kempe initially sought an ecclesiastical career, but fearing his stammer would blight this choice he turned instead to the decoration of churches, learning much about medieval art from time working with Morris and the architect George Frederick Bodley. He was influenced by Renaissance artists from sixteenth-century Germany and The Netherlands as well as by the late-fifteenth-century stained glass at St Mary's Church, Fairford, Gloucestershire, which remarkably survived the destruction of the Reformation and Civil War and today still forms the most complete set of medieval windows in England. His style was characterised by intricate drawings often set upon clear and yellow stained glass, with limited sections of dark colours like olive green and ruby red. Some windows contain a single important figure richly adorned in bejewelled robes and patterned fabrics with softly shaded grey faces standing beneath an intricately designed medieval canopy. Other windows with traditional Christian themes have figures arranged in pairs and groups, with Kempe's remarkable attention to detail in both the foreground and background, sometimes including a beautiful landscape viewed through a window. His studio produced a prodigious quantity of stained glass up until the 1930s, maintaining the fine detailing and ample use of clear and yellow stained glass.

Another leading designer who championed the aesthetic style in stained glass was Daniel Cottier. Born in Glasgow, he received training from James Ballantine and spent time in London, where he was influenced by Morris, Rossetti and Ford Madox Brown. On returning to Scotland, he worked briefly for Field and Allan of Leith before establishing his own studio and taking on another talented Scottish designer, Stephen Adam. Like his mentors, Cottier rejected the busy, formal arrangement of figures and Gothic motifs of the 1860s for a lighter, clearer style with large, lively and expressive figures donned in robes and swags, often surrounded by clear glass featuring yellow-stained foliage and flowers. Stephen Adam became a successful designer during this period after leaving Cottier's studio to establish his own business in 1870. His mosaics of coloured glass have several tones of a restrained colour palette, with beautifully simple figure work highlighted by black leaded lines. Adam created windows with Classical-style figures, dramatic colouring and foliage motifs that bridge the gap between the romantic

One of the finest collections of Kempe windows can be found at Wakefield Cathedral, Yorkshire, many with his wheatsheaf emblem in the border. This close up shows a contemporary Victorian gentleman dressed in gleaming armour of silver and gold.

The Church of St Martin of Tours, Saundby, Nottinghamshire, has an impressive set of C.E. Kempe windows, which can be viewed from close quarters. Note the beautifully detailed landscapes viewed through the windows.

OPPOSITE
Although the form of this window was similar to those from previous decades, this example from the 1870s by Clayton and Bell displays the more restrained colour palette and darker tones combined with clear glass for the faces which were now fashionable.

aesthetic designs of the 1870s and the striking colours and simple linework of the early twentieth century.

Although the number of new churches being built tapered off, the demand for memorial glass for existing edifices and foreign commissions kept the production lines of established studios and glazing firms busy. Much of this work was still in a Gothic Revival style and could lack originality not just because cartoons were repeatedly re-used to save time and money, but also because the design had to be approved by the family of the deceased and the church clergy, who were usually conservative in outlook and comfortable choosing an established style. Despite this there were some elements of leading designers' work which began influencing mass-produced designs, and generally the standard of drawing and quality of glass improved during the late nineteenth century. Windows began integrating clear glass, which enhanced the central colour image and also allowed more light into the church. Figures became more realistic, with contemporary faces now on clear glass in place of the muddy pinks that had formerly been used, and in natural poses rather than stylised medieval forms. Some still used primary colours, but more restrained tertiary colours became fashionable, such as rich purple, olive green, claret red, saffron and browns, with backgrounds of detailed foliage in shades of green and blue. Windows featuring two levels representing heaven above earth were popular, while the traditional Gothic form of a figure below a canopy was still widely used, although the architectural details were usually lighter and greater in refinement. During this highpoint of Victorian stained glass there is much to admire and enjoy from the works of all qualities that were produced for the church. Perhaps the greatest change in this period was that this colourful art form now became the height of fashion in the home.

BELOW RIGHT This window by Burlison and Grylls from the early 1890s shows the fashion for earthy tones with browns, yellows and golds making a stark contrast to the bright colours of the previous generation.

STAINED GLASS FOR THE MASSES: 1860–1930

STAINED GLASS WAS never the sole reserve of the church. Medieval and Tudor nobles had their family coats of arms installed in prominent windows, and this was revived in the first half of the nineteenth century in fashionable romantic castles and mock Elizabethan mansions. As the Gothic Revival began to inspire the design of large houses from the 1850s, mosaics of coloured glass began to appear as key elements in their windows and doors. Victorians with money earned from industry and commerce bought up old country seats and had stained glass coats of arms or portraits of their ancestors installed in their new homes in order to create some legitimacy to their family's new position. Alternatively, new coloured glass designs in fashionable Gothic or Arts and Crafts styles could be incorporated in windows to display the owner's refined taste. They could also express their personal interests, desires and ambitions by featuring medieval heroes, classical tragedies or industrious endeavours. Stained glass in these grand Victorian houses is therefore not just a decorative feature, but can tell us something about the personality of the person who commissioned it.

Commissions also came from commercial businesses, as companies wishing to appear fashionable and modern built their new offices and showrooms in the latest architectural style. Stained glass was viewed as a modern and colourful piece of decorative art that could express the ambitions or heritage of a business. New stations and hotels built to serve

OPPOSITE
When Lady Waldegrave inherited Horace Walpole's Strawberry Hill, she installed heraldic glass in the round drawing room window pictured here. What had been eccentric in Walpole's day was now in the 1860s the height of fashion.

OPPOSITE
The Butterfield
Family were mill
owners who
bought an old
country seat
near Keighley,
West Yorkshire,
and built
Cliffe Castle,
a fashionable
Gothic mansion.
This stained glass
window features
family members
in Tudor dress,
seemingly an
attempt to imply
they were of
ancient lineage.

the expanding railway network could feature patterned glass designs in the ironwork canopies that covered their grand entrances, often advertising the name of the business or the areas it covered. Theatres, banks, public houses and shops also used stained glass windows as fashionable displays. During the late Victorian period, large public corporations and councils were established; they were quick to express their new-found confidence and ambition with impressive public buildings featuring large windows with coats of arms of important dignitaries or symbols of local industry and commerce.

Such was the popularity of stained glass that it worked its way down to the modest middle-class suburban home. Builders erected rows of standard terraces and then added some fashionable flourishes to try to attract a higher class of tenant, including stained glass panels in doors, fanlights and

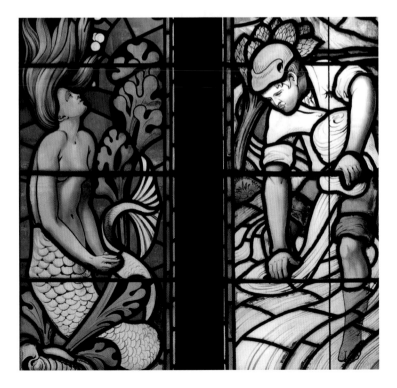

This unique
stained glass was
installed as part
of an Arts and
Crafts makeover
of an old
house in Leek,
Staffordshire.
The mermaid
was part of a
local legend,
while the man
handling cloth
represented
a major local
industry.

windows. Not only did they add extra light to brighten the hallway and landing with warm sparkling colours, but they also kept the household out of sight of prying eyes, an important consideration to Victorian families who valued their privacy. Most of this glazing for domestic use was mass produced and sold via catalogues or showrooms. A border around a sash window made of deep red or blue glass with star shapes in the corner was popular in the early to mid-nineteenth century. Glazed front

LEFT
Cliffe Castle Museum features a unique collection of Victorian stained glass, including excellent examples by William Morris as featured here. Morris and Co's domestic glass often featured heroic characters, musicians, romances and tales of death and glory.

ABOVE LEFT
The sunflower
was a popular
motif in the
1880s, as here
at Papplewick
Pumping Station,
Nottinghamshire.

ABOVE RIGHT
Textured glass
was fashionable
in the late
nineteenth and
early twentieth
centuries, as in
this Art Nouveau
example
at Buxton
Opera House,
Derbyshire.

doors with two tall stained glass panels became fashionable from the 1870s. Some had colourful geometric patterns, often featuring a bullseye or bullion – the raised centre point of a disc of spun glass – a simple type that remained popular until the start of the First World War. A more impressive option included a central round, square or lozenge-shaped piece with a painted design of a landscape, birds, flowers or foliage, which was fashionable in the 1870s and '80s. Later nineteenth-century versions typically have a single design in leaded glass filling the panel, with stylised foliage and flowers the most common theme. Around this time textured glass began to be incorporated into panels where a pattern was machine pressed into the glazing during manufacture.

The best windows and door panels in Victorian houses featured coloured glass patterns with a decorative roundel in the centre, featuring flora, fauna, landscape or, as in this example, a romanticised portrait.

By the turn of the twentieth century, stained glass could also be found in the upper sections of fashionable casement windows, with stylised floral designs, swags or simple heraldic symbols popular motifs. After the First World War decorative glass remained popular in doors and windows, sometimes featuring cheerful scenes of bright, colourful sailing ships, rolling hills, windmills, trees and a rising sun. Although stylised foliage and swags remained popular in the 1930s, windows and doors increasingly had Art Deco geometric designs formed from clear textured or coloured glass, some with sunrays in golden tones to appeal to the more fashion-conscious homeowner. These daring new designs reflected the changes that had been made in the decorative arts since the turn of the century, as windows of incredible richness with a skilful control of light made for a memorable final evolution of Victorian stained glass.

OPPOSITE
This beautiful Art Nouveau stylised tree and floral design features above the entrance to the Royal Arcade, Norwich, designed by George Skipper and opened in 1899.

WHALL, CLARKE AND STRACHAN: 1900–1930

IN THE OPENING decades of the twentieth century, stained glass remained a vibrant and innovative art form. Improvements in standards and techniques had been driven by the next generation of stained glass artists who had been educated within new art schools, which had mostly been established in the 1880s and '90s. The first generation of Victorian stained glass designers had been largely self-taught or had developed their skills from other trades, the second had trained with established companies or architects before going out alone, but this generation had received teaching specifically for the art from its finest exponents. They had time to experiment and develop their skills, resulting in sparkling, opulent pieces of work in stylish new designs that stand out from traditional medieval-style windows that were still being mass produced by the old Victorian glazing companies.

Some of the finest pieces produced by this generation were in response to the trauma of the First World War and the need to commemorate the catastrophic loss of life. A vast number of stained glass windows were produced to satisfy this demand, often featuring St George, St Michael or the Good Shepherd and an epitaph below recording the tragic story of soldiers who never returned. This turned out to be the last flourish of Victorian stained glass, as economic strife in the late 1920s and changing fashions resulted in many glazing companies and studios closing their doors for good.

OPPOSITE
A sumptuous and glistening window from 1923 by Harry Clarke, at St Mary's Church, Nantwich, Cheshire. The distinctive elongated and placid figures represent Saint Cecilia, the Virgin Mary and Richard the Lionheart.

Cathedral cloisters were often glazed after the First World War to create additional windows for memorials. This example from Worcester showing Bishop John Hooper, who was burnt at the stake under orders of Queen Mary, contains innovative painting effects and hand-made glass.

Designers in this period had access to or the knowledge to make a wider range of glass types and colours by which they could create new effects to alter the way windows refracted light and enhance the design. The medieval skill of flashing glass by coating it in a colour to make a more translucent tone was used especially on folded fabric. A new type of glass had been introduced, which was made by blowing the molten material into a rectangular-shaped mould and then cutting it down the corners, leaving pieces of glass that were thicker in the centre. This richly textured Norman slab glass with bubbles and swirls made interesting patterns in the light and was often used by Arts and Crafts designers. Streaky glass with different tones or colours running through it was used within some designs in the early twentieth century, as was plated glass with two pieces sandwiched together to create different effects. Tertiary colours such as saffron, amber, teal, as well as pinks, browns, bright greens, rich purples and dark reds were especially popular. In the finest windows of this age these different qualities and colours of glass, combined with various paint effects and a very dark background, resulted in designs that glowed and sparkled with light.

Of all those designers who embraced the ideals of the Arts and Crafts movement Christopher Whall is the shining light. He was a talented artist who not only designed stained glass but also learnt how to make the raw material and piece the windows together. He emphasised the importance of this control of his art through his teaching and influential book which would inspire a generation. Whall was educated at the Royal Academy Schools and spent three years studying art and architecture in Italy, but by the time he was thirty his career was floundering and he was broke. After spending time as a lay member of a religious community, he took up illustration work for various publications and began designing stained glass windows, including commissions for James Powell and Sons. Whall married the portrait painter Florence Chaplin, and the couple set up home in Dorking where he established his own studio in an old shed. Here he could carry out all aspects of the craft, from the firing of the glass through to the leading of the window now that commissions finally began to roll in. He also took on teaching roles at the Central School of Arts and Crafts in London, founded in 1896, and at the Royal College of Art. Whall was always keen to experiment and develop the art, and his style varied over the years.

Memorial windows raised to remember those killed in the First World War are important records of this tragic human loss. This example, by Burlison and Grylls from St John the Baptist Church, Coventry, features the four patron saints of England, Scotland, Wales and Ireland.

This image of Christ by Christopher Whall was installed in 1899 at St Martin's Church, Low Marple, Manchester. Note the movement in the piece due to his vibrant drawing style and the effects created by the paint and hand-made glass.

He used different types of glass to make windows full of texture, lighting effects and glorious colour, and unlike many of his contemporaries he also used clear glass in his designs. His figures often have softly textured skin with roughly drawn hair full of movement with dark paint and innovative leading highlighting details from expressive hands to stormy seas. Whall's talented daughter Veronica worked with him during his later years and continued the studio's production after he died in 1924, becoming an important designer in her own right.

Women had played a minor role in the production of Victorian stained glass, but all that was to change from the 1890s. Mary Lowndes was one of the first female designers of stained glass windows and a pioneer for women in the trade. After training at the Slade School of Art, London, she became an assistant for Henry Holiday but spent much of her time learning all aspects of stained glass design so she could start producing her own work. It was Christopher Whall who encouraged her to establish her own workshop, and with assistance from Alfred John Drury they established Lowndes and Drury, which provided Arts and Crafts designers with the facilities to make their own windows. Their site in Lettice Street, Fulham, named the Glass House, still stands today. Her work has a vibrant, sometimes sketchy drawing style, with the figures standing out by the use of prominent leading and clear glass. Lowndes was also prominent in the suffragette movement, designing many of the iconic posters associated with the cause.

Margaret Agnes Rope excelled at the Birmingham School of Art and from 1911 worked at the Glass House, producing a number of colourful, passionately religious windows until she became a Carmelite nun in 1923. Her cousin Margaret Edith Rope worked with her at the Glass House on a number of windows and was more prolific in her output. Mabel Esplin was another promising stained glass designer based at the Glass House. Her first major commission was for a series of windows at All Saint's Cathedral, now the Republican Palace Museum, in Khartoum; however, her assistant Joan Fulleylove had to complete the work as Esplin's health deteriorated and she suffered a breakdown that ended her career. Wilhelmina Geddes began designing windows in Ireland before moving to London in 1925 to work at the Glass House. This leading Irish artist was a meticulous perfectionist, with her striking and colourful windows featuring figures drawn with a vigorous anatomical eye, with heavy shading revealing every muscle and vein. Her later work marks the transition from the historically inspired Victorian designs to the modernism that would dominate post Second World War windows.

Much of Geddes' early work was produced in Dublin at An Túr Gloine, the Tower of Glass. Edward Martyn, a playwright and later the first President of Sinn Féin, was a passionate supporter of the Irish arts. After having to order stained glass from Christopher Whall in England for his family church as domestic products were of indifferent quality, he set about establishing a facility in

A close up of the Archangel Michael, part of a memorial window by Christopher and Veronica Whall dating from 1923 at Worcester Cathedral. Note how the rough vibrancy in the shining armour contrasts with the delicate stippled face and hands.

his home country to rectify the situation. Along with Sarah Purser, a portrait painter who had made her fortune from investing in Guinness, they established their new stained glass workshop in 1903, with Purser insisting that they should follow Arts and Crafts doctrine, stating, 'Each window is the work of one artist who makes the sketch and cartoon and selects and paints every morsel of glass him or herself.' Whall's assistant, Alfred Child, was the manager of An Túr Gloine and naturally his mentor's philosophy was imparted on those who worked there, including Michael Healy, Wilhelmina Geddes and her pupil Evie Hone.

At the same time as this key co-operative workshop was influencing the art, so another talented stained glass designer from Ireland was making his mark. Harry Clarke had taken evening classes with Alfred Child at the Dublin School of Art, while he spent his days helping in his father's church-decorating business, which he and his brother would continue to run after the latter's death in 1921. His incredible gift for illustration can be seen in both his stained glass, of which he produced over 150 commissions, and his breathtakingly detailed and imaginative book illustrations. His windows feature characteristic wide-eyed, ethereal figures dressed in beautifully decorated robes and armour set against richly coloured backgrounds filled with stylised flora and fauna. As with other leading stained glass artists of the time, his technical ability to control the lighting effect on each single piece of glass gives his beautiful artwork a sparkling extra dimension that needs to be seen in the flesh.

In Scotland during the 1880s and '90s, the Glasgow School of Art developed from an establishment with an undistinguished traditional approach to become a centre of modern decorative arts, including stained glass design. Its roll call of students included Charles Rennie Mackintosh, James Herbert McNair and the sisters Margaret and Frances Macdonald. Mackintosh's Art Nouveau stylised floral designs with sinuous, elongated stalks are instantly recognisable and much replicated in domestic and commercial settings. Alf Webster was another exciting prospect to benefit from the Glasgow School in which he enrolled in 1903. He was trained by Stephen Adam, whom he worked alongside and then took over the reins of his company on his master's death in 1910. Webster began developing his own style with bold colouring, but he died from injuries sustained in action during the First World War.

Douglas Strachan, the leading Scottish stained glass designer of this period, received his training at Gray's School of Art, Aberdeen, and The Royal Scottish Academy, Edinburgh. However, it was after a tour studying the medieval and

Renaissance art of France and Italy that he started to develop his personal style. Like Harry Clarke he was especially fascinated by the glass in Chartres Cathedral, Strachan's daughter later writing in her memoir that it was the windows' 'luminous monumentality rather than specific details of style and technique' that inspired him. His vibrant designs used white glass alongside glorious colours, imaginative shapes in the lead, and serious-looking figures, with his later Art Deco-style faces having rough, chiselled features. His great works include windows at the Peace Palace in The Hague, Netherlands, and the Scottish National War Memorial in Edinburgh Castle.

St Margaret of Scotland is depicted in this 1922 window by Douglas Strachan in the chapel named after her within Edinburgh Castle.

A characteristic Edwardian window by James Crofts Powell of James Powell and Sons, in memory of Sir Douglas Galton. Note the Art Nouveau style detailing on the leg armour and the fashionable dark purple, olive green and crimson red glass.

These great windows designed by Whall, Strachan, Clarke and other leading designers in the early twentieth century mark the culmination of the development of Victorian stained glass. The transition from the brightly coloured medieval-style windows of the 1850s to the sparkling masterpieces of the 1920s is fascinating to view. The combination of art, science and industry brought together to make such colourful and expressive creations in glass reflects the great changes in the field of decorative art and design during this period. Perhaps most exciting of all is that these bejewelled pieces of Victorian art are freely available to view in cathedrals and churches across England, Wales, Scotland and Ireland, although binoculars or a camera with a long

zoom is useful to fully appreciate them. Windows can also be studied in a number of museums across the country, including the V&A in London and the Stained Glass Museum in Ely Cathedral, where you can witness every brush stroke and bubble in the glass at close quarters.

Despite a growing appreciation of Britain's Victorian stained glass heritage, much of it is under threat. Many of the windows, especially those from the early years, were made using experimental glass and paints, and the fading and weathering of the design is a common problem that requires specialist and expensive repair. Protecting the windows also presents problems, as an external mesh of wire may be effective at

A First World War memorial window at All Saints Church, Stamford, Lincolnshire, with the epitaph stating 'To the Glorious and undying memory of those from this Parish who died in the Great War, (1914–1918), that England might live'.

preventing damage but also casts unpleasant shadows across the artwork. There are more sympathetic solutions, but these come at a price. Many churches would appreciate funds to help restore their works of art, which they endeavour to keep accessible to all visitors.

At a more humble level, Victorian stained glass doors and windows are still being ripped out of homes each year to be replaced by unsympathetic modern types on the incorrect assumption that the superior-quality originals cannot be upgraded for energy efficiency or security. These geometric or floral glazed patterns are a key part of the history of a home, reflecting fashionable styles and the ambitions of its builder or owner, and their loss devalues a period property. Watching the sun rise and sparkle in pieces of old coloured and textured glass while it casts a dazzling display on the interior makes the effort of maintaining them a worthwhile endeavour.

FURTHER READING

Barlow, Adrian. *Kempe: The Life, Art and Legacy of Charles Eamer Kempe*. Lutterworth Press, 2018.

Cheshire, Jim. *Stained Glass and the Victorian Gothic Revival*. Manchester University Press, 2004.

Costigan, Lucy and Cullen, Martin. *Strangest Genius: The Stained Glass of Harry Clarke*. The History Press Ireland, 2010.

Harries, John and Hicks, Carola. *Discovering Stained Glass*. Shire, 2006.

Harrison, Martin. *Victorian Stained Glass*. Barrie and Jenkins, 1980.

MacCarthy, Fiona. *William Morris: A Life for Our Time*. Faber and Faber, 1994.

McRae Thomson, Aidan. *Stained Glass*. Amberley, 2018.

Osborne, June. *Stained Glass in England*. Alan Sutton, 1993.

Shepherd, Stanley. *The Stained Glass of A.W.N. Pugin*. Spire Books, 2009.

Smith, Alison. *Edward Burne-Jones*. Tate Publishing, 2018.

Stavridi, Margaret. *Master of Glass: Charles Eamer Kempe, 1837–1907*. John Taylor Book Ventures, 1988.

Waters, William and Carew-Cox, Alistair. *Angels & Icons: Pre-Raphaelite Stained Glass 1850–1870*. Seraphim Press, 2012.

Waters, William and Carew-Cox, Alistair. *Damozels & Deities: Pre-Raphaelite Stained Glass 1870–1898*. Seraphim Press, 2017.

Yorke, Trevor. *Gothic Revival Architecture*. Shire, 2017.

PLACES TO VISIT

Bath Abbey, Bath, BA1 1LT. Telephone: 01225 422462. Website: www.bathabbey.org This imposing edifice in the centre of the Georgian city is full of Victorian stained glass by Ward and Hughes, Burlison and Grylls, J. Powell and Sons, the Chance Brothers and most notably Clayton and Bell, who produced the huge east and west windows.

Birmingham Anglican Cathedral, Colmore Row, Birmingham, B3 2QB. Telephone: 0121 262 1840. Website: www.birminghamcathedral.com Four moving and memorable examples of the work of Edward Burne-Jones and Morris and Co. The three east windows depict the Nativity, Ascension and Crucifixion, with the Last Judgement in the west window.

Birmingham Catholic Cathedral, St Chads Queensway, Birmingham, B4 6EY. Telephone: 0121 230 6211. Website: www.stchadscathedral.org.uk One of Pugin's major commissions with stained glass windows, including those in the chancel by William Warrington. The cathedral is the starting point of The Birmingham Pugin Trail, which includes Birmingham Museum and Library, which holds the records and drawings of John Hardman and Sons.

Blatherwycke, Holy Trinity Church, Main Street, Blatherwycke, Northamptonshire, PE8 6YW. Telephone: 07876 324554. Website: www.visitchurches. org.uk/visit/church-listing/holy-trinity-blatherwycke. html Attractively set little church with a good selection of different types of stained glass, including work by Heaton, Butler and Bayne, Clayton and Bell, Gibbs and C.E. Kempe (Churches Conservation Trust).

Bradford Cathedral, 1 Stott Hill, Bradford, West Yorkshire, BD1 4EH. Telephone: 01274 777720. Website: www.bradfordcathedral.org

This window by Christopher Whall at St John the Baptist Church, Burford, Oxfordshire, dates from 1907 and is enhanced by the use of clear glass to frame the figures. His finest collection can be seen at Gloucester Cathedral.

Good range of Victorian glass from leading designers, including Morris and Co.

Burford, St John the Baptist Church, Church Green, Burford, Oxfordshire, OX18 4RY. Telephone: 01993 823788. Website: www.burfordchurch.org An historical treasure trove which has windows by Kempe and Whall.

Cheadle, St Giles' Catholic Church, 18 Charles Street, Cheadle, Stoke-on-Trent, ST10 1ED. Telephone: 01538 753130. Website: www.stgilescheadle.org.uk Outstanding example of Pugin's Gothic interior design with his stained glass windows produced by William Wailes.

Chester Cathedral, St Werburgh Street, Chester, CH1 2DY. Telephone: 01244 324756. Website: www.chestercathedral.com A very good collection of Victorian stained glass from numerous studios. The glass in the cloisters can be studied at close quarters.

Chichester Cathedral, Chichester, West Sussex, PO19 1PX. Telephone: 01243 782595. Website: www.chichestercathedral.org.uk Good selection of early Victorian windows.

Cliffe Castle Museum, Spring Gardens Lane, Keighley, West Yorkshire, BD20 6LH. Telephone: 01535 618231. Website: www.bradfordmuseums.org/venues/cliffe-castle-museum Excellent exhibition of Victorian stained glass, including important pieces by William Morris as well as an impressive Gothic window above the main staircase.

Ely Cathedral, Ely, Cambridgeshire, CB7 4DL.
Telephone: 01353 667735. Website: www.elycathedral.
org The Stained Glass Museum within the building is
a fantastic starting point for anyone wishing to learn
more about the subject. You can study glass from leading
designers at close quarters in this simply laid out and
informative museum. In addition, the cathedral itself has
perhaps the best collection of early Victorian stained glass.

Falinge, St Edmund's Church, Edmund Street, Rochdale,
Greater Manchester, OL12 6QF. Telephone: 0845 303
2760. Website: www.visitchurches.org.uk/visit/church-
listing/st-edmund-falinge.html An excellent example of
Victorian architecture from the 1870s with a series of
windows by Lavers, Barraud and Westlake.

Gloucester Cathedral, College Green, Gloucester, GL1 2LX.
Telephone: 01452 528095. Website:
www.gloucestercathedral.org.uk
A good range of Victorian
windows in addition to the
outstanding examples by
Christopher Whall.

Halifax Minster, Dispensary
Walk, Halifax, West Yorkshire,
HX1 1QR. Telephone: 01422
355436. Website:
www.halifaxminster.org.uk
The east window is one of
the best examples of George
Hedgeland's enamel-painted glass
along with examples from other
Victorian studios.

Hereford Cathedral, Cathedral
Close, Hereford,
Herefordshire, HR1 2NG.
Telephone: 01432 374200.

The magnificent east window at Halifax Minster by George Hedgeland from 1855. The piece is somewhat outdated for this period, with the use of enamel painting, distorted architectural canopies and a rather haphazard application of colour.

Website: www.herefordcathedral.org A fine selection
of Victorian stained glass along with some excellent
modern counterparts.

Leek, St Edward's Church, Leek, Staffordshire, ST13 6AB.
Telephone: 01538 388134. Website: www.leekparish.
org.uk Good collection of Victorian windows, including
some by Morris and Co. Also All Saints Church, Leek,
ST13 5PT, an Arts and Crafts church with more excellent
stained glass, and St Edward's Church, Hollow Lane,
Cheddleton, Leek, ST13 7HP, in which you can see the
progression in style of Morris windows.

Lincoln Cathedral, Minster Yard, Lincoln,
LN2 1PX. Telephone: 01522 561600.
Website: www.lincolncathedral.com This outstanding
and spectacular cathedral contains excellent examples
of Victorian windows, especially from the early
Victorian period.

London, Holy Trinity Sloane Square, Sloane Street,
London, SW1X 9BZ. Telephone: 020 7730 7270.
Website: www.sloanechurch.org Architecturally important
Arts and Crafts church with excellent stained glass
including the east window by Morris and Co.

Marple, St Martin's Church, Brabyns Brow, Low Marple,
Manchester, SK6 5DT. Website: www.stmartins-
lowmarple.co.uk This charming Arts and Crafts church
contains excellent stained glass by Christopher Whall and
Morris and Co among others.

Newcastle Cathedral, St Nicholas Square, Newcastle, Tyne
and Wear, NE1 1PF. Website: www.newcastlecathedral.
org.uk Good range of stained glass from the nineteenth
and twentieth centuries, including work by William
Wailes, who was based in the city.

Norwich Cathedral, The Close, Norwich, Norfolk,
NR1 4DH. Telephone: 01603 218300.
Website: www.cathedral.org.uk Very good selection

of Victorian stained glass, including the impressive George Hedgeland west window. Useful tool for viewing all the windows at www.norwich-heritage.co.uk.

Peterborough Cathedral, Peterborough, Cambridgeshire, PE1 1XS. Telephone: 01733 355315. Website: www.peterborough-cathedral.org.uk Fascinating range of early Victorian stained glass, including a window designed by Rossetti.

Redbourne, St Andrew's Church, Redbourne, Gainsborough, Lincolnshire, DN21 4QN. Telephone: 0845 303 2760. Website: www.visitchurches.org.uk/visit/church-listing/st-andrew-redbourne.html Features rare enamel-painted stained glass, including the stunning Day of Judgement east window dating from the 1830s (Churches Conservation Trust).

St Edmundsbury Cathedral, Angel Hill, Bury St Edmunds, Suffolk, IP33 1LS. Telephone: 01284 748720. Website: www.stedscathedral.org Impressive collection of Victorian stained glass, including some early examples from William Warrington and William Wailes.

Salisbury Cathedral, The Close, Salisbury, Wiltshire, SP1 2EF. Telephone: 01722 555120. Website: www.salisburycathedral.org.uk A varied range of glass, including the rare eighteenth-century enamel-painted Brazen Serpent in the Wilderness by James Pearson.

Saundby, Church of St Martin of Tours, Gainsborough Road, East Retford, Nottinghamshire, DN22 9ER.

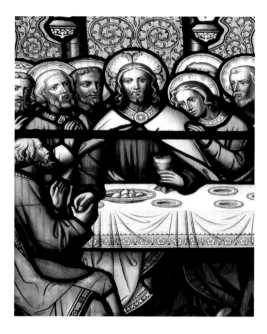

This window in Peterborough Cathedral from 1858 has heavily shaded faces and a patterned pale blue background, which are a throwback to enamel-painted windows, but the coloured glass cut into shapes to complement the design is more cutting edge.

Telephone: 0845 303 2760. Website: www.visitchurches. org.uk/visit/church-listing/st-martin-saundby.html An excellent series of stained glass windows by Charles Kempe from the 1880s (Churches Conservation Trust).

Scarborough, St Martin-on-the-Hill Church, Albion Road, Scarborough, YO11 2BT. Website: www.friendsofstmartins.co.uk An outstanding Victorian church interior with much of the decoration and stained glass by Morris, Burne-Jones, Rossetti, Webb and Madox Brown.

Selsley, All Saints, Selsley, Gloucestershire, GL5 5LG. Website: www.allsaintsselsley.org.uk A restrained Victorian church with an excellent series of stained glass windows by Morris, Marshall and Faulkner.

Stamford, St John the Baptist, Stamford, St John's Street, Stamford, Lincolnshire, PE9 2DB. Telephone: 0845 303 2760. Website: www.visitchurches.org.uk/visit/church-listing/st-john-stamford.html A fine range of Victorian windows in this medieval edifice (Churches Conservation Trust) and in the nearby All Saints Church, All Saints Place, Stamford, PE9 2AG.

Studley Royal, St Mary's Church, Church Walk, Studley Royal, Ripon, North Yorkshire, HG4 3DY. Telephone: 01765 608888. Website: www.english-heritage.org.uk/visit/places/st-marys-church-studley-royal Stained glass windows form part of this stunningly colourful interior by William Burges (English Heritage/National Trust).

Truro Cathedral, St Mary's Street, Truro, Cornwall, TR1 2AF. Telephone: 01872 276782. Website: www.trurocathedral.org.uk Impressive late Victorian cathedral with a largely complete range of stained glass windows conceived as a single project and executed by Clayton and Bell. Probably the largest single commission from the period.

V&A Museum, Cromwell Road, South Kensington, London, SW7 2RL. Telephone: 020 7942 2000. Website: www.vam.ac.uk Important display of the finest Victorian stained glass. A huge range of images, drawings and cartoons can also be accessed via the collections tab on the website.

Wakefield Cathedral, Northgate, Wakefield, South Yorkshire, WF1 1HG. Telephone: 01924 373923. Website: www.wakefieldcathedral.org.uk Impressive collection of stained glass by C.E. Kempe. Look out for his wheatsheaf symbol in the bottom left of some windows.

William Morris Gallery, Lloyd Park, Forest Road, Walthamstow, London, E17 4PP. Telephone: 020 8496 4390. Website: www.wmgallery.org.uk Collection of William Morris artwork and artefacts including stained glass and cartoons.

Winchester Cathedral, The Close, Winchester, Hampshire, SO23 9LS. Telephone: 01962 857200. Website: www.winchester-cathedral.org.uk Good selection of Victorian stained glass, including examples from Morris and Co and C.E. Kempe.

Worcester Cathedral, College Yard, Worcester, Worcestershire, WR1 2LA. Telephone: 01905 732900. Website: www.worcestercathedral.co.uk Impressive range of Victorian windows, including examples from John Hardman, Clayton and Bell, Burlison and Grylls, J. Powell and Sons, Lavers and Barraud, and Christopher and Veronica Whall.

INDEX